SECRET HISTORY

THE COLD WAR

THE
COLD
WAR

R. G. GRANT

ARCTURUS

This edition first published by Arcturus Publishing
Distributed by Black Rabbit Books
P.O. Box 3263
Mankato
Minnesota MN 56002

Printed in China

The right of R. G. Grant to be identified
as the author of this work has been asserted
by him in accordance with the Copyright,
Designs and Patents Act 1988.

Series concept: Alex Woolf
Editors: Karen Taschek and Alex Woolf
Designer: Tall Tree
Picture researcher: Alex Woolf

Library of Congress Cataloging-in-Publication Data

Grant, R. G.
   The Cold War / Reg Grant.
      p. cm. – (Secret history)
   Includes index.
   Summary: "This high-interest series, aimed at reluctant
readers, looks at secret campaigns behind the major
conflicts of the past 100 years. Biographical sidebars
focus on heroic or notorious personalities. Highlighted
fact features include special operations and their results,
resistance movements, propaganda and the history of
the time - as is known....and not readily known"-
Provided by publisher.
   ISBN 978-1-84837-696-0 (library binding)
   1. Cold War–Juvenile literature. I. Title.
   D843.G715 2011
   909.82'5–dc22
                        2010011765

SL000970US   Supplier 03 Date 0510

Picture credits:
Corbis: cover *top left* (Swim Ink 2, LLC), cover *right*
(Bettmann), 6 (Bettmann), 7 (Bettmann), 8 (Bettmann),
9 (Bettmann), 10 (Bettmann), 11 (Rykoff Collection),
12 (George Steinmetz), 13 (Bettmann), 14 (Bettmann),
15 (Bettmann), 19 *top* (Roger Ressmeyer), 19 *bottom*
(Bettmann), 20 (Bettmann), 21 (Bettmann), 25 (Bettmann),
26 (Museum of Flight), 27 (Bettmann), 28 (Bettmann),
29 (Bettmann), 30 (Bettmann), 32 (epa), 33 (Claude
Urraca/Sygma), 34 (Bettmann), 37 (Bettmann), 38
(Bill Gentile), 39 (Reza/Webistan), 40 (Bettmann), 42
(Martin Athenstaedt/epa), 43 (David Brauchli/Reuters).
Getty Images: 16 (Michael Grecco), 17 (Evening
Standard/Hulton Archive), 22 *left and right*
(Keystone/Hulton Archive), 23 *top and bottom*
(Keystone/Hulton Archive), 24 (Paul Schultzer/Time &
Life Pictures), 31 (Jean-Claude Delmas/
AFP), 35 (Rolls Press/Popperfoto), 36 (Larry Burrows/
Time & Life Pictures), 41 (Keystone/Hulton Archive).
Shutterstock: *binoculars* cover (Dmitry Suzdalev).

Cover illustrations: *top left*: Soviet propaganda poster
from 1961; *right*: CIA director William Colby
(1973–1976); *bottom left*: Cold War–era binoculars.

Spread heading illustrations are all from Shutterstock:
6, 24, 28: binoculars (Dmitry Suzdalev); 8, 12: bomb
(fckncg); 10, 14, 42: missile (mmaxer); 16, 32, 36:
helmet (EchoArt); 18, 30: sunglasses (Robnroll); 20,
22: camera (Mikhail Pogosov); 26, 40: satellite
(Pinchuk Alexey); 34, 38: gun (RCPPHOTO).

Every attempt has been made to clear copyright.
Should there be any inadvertent omission, please
apply to the publisher for rectification.

CONTENTS

FROM ALLIES TO ENEMIES

The Cold War was a long struggle for global supremacy between the two superpowers, the United States and the Soviet Union, and their allies. It was called the "Cold War" because the superpowers never fought each other openly on a battlefield. Instead, they attacked each other in underhand ways, through spying, propaganda, secret operations, and guerrilla wars.

DIFFERENT SYSTEMS

The United States and the Soviet Union had fought as allies against Nazi Germany in World War II. But after the Germans were defeated in 1945, the victors soon had a falling out. The United States and the communist Soviet Union had very different political systems and beliefs. The Soviet Union saw the United States as an aggressive imperialist country. The United States saw Soviet communism as a threat to freedom and democracy.

Inhabitants of communist-ruled East Germany and pro-American West Germany stand on opposite sides of the fence that divided their country early in the Cold War. Over time, the border was strengthened with minefields and watchtowers.

By 1949, Europe was divided by an "Iron Curtain." To the east of the curtain were countries occupied by Soviet troops and with Soviet-style communist regimes. To the west, countries such as Britain, France, and Italy joined the United States in the anti-Soviet NATO alliance. In Asia, the United States failed to stop China from becoming a communist country under Mao Ze Dong.

PLAYING HOT AND COLD

The hostility between the two sides was intense. The Korean War (see panel) was only the first of many "hot wars" that were fought between communists and anti-communists. But the superpowers learned to play a dangerous game, arming themselves to the teeth with the most destructive weapons ever built but always pulling back from the brink of total war.

THE KOREAN WAR

In 1950, North Korea, a communist-ruled state backed by the Soviet Union and China, invaded US-backed South Korea. The United States and its allies waged a three-year war against North Korean and Chinese troops. Around four million lives were lost, but the war remained limited. It was fought only on the Korean peninsula and nuclear weapons were not used.

US Marines, with a bazooka and a machine gun, prepare to take on communist troops during the Korean War. Almost 34,000 US soldiers died in the course of the war.

IN THEIR OWN WORDS

In a speech in the United States in 1946, Winston Churchill, who had been Britain's prime minister during World War II, warned that Europe was being divided between the communist east and democratic west:

From Stettin in the Baltic to Trieste in the Adriatic an iron curtain has descended across the continent [Europe].

From a speech given at Fulton, Missouri, on March 5, 1946

THE BIG SECRET

At the start of the Cold War, the United States was the only country in the world with nuclear weapons. The United States had dropped two atom bombs on Japan in 1945. Each one destroyed a whole city. The Soviet Union was determined to catch up with the United States. Atom bombs became the focus of a desperate arms race.

ATOM BOMB PROJECTS

The United States developed the atom bomb during World War II. The project was cloaked in secrecy, but the Soviet Union was kept informed about it by its spies (see pages 20–21). The Soviets set up their own atom bomb project in 1944. They exploded their first "A-bomb" in 1949.

The United States rushed to develop an even more destructive nuclear weapon, the hydrogen bomb, to keep ahead of the Soviets. In 1952, the United States exploded an "H-bomb" at Enewetak Atoll in the Pacific. It was

In November 1952, the United States tested a hydrogen bomb on Enewetak Atoll in the Pacific Ocean that sent a mushroom cloud towering over 18 miles (30 kilometers) into the air. The explosion totally destroyed the island of Elugelab, turning it into a bomb crater.

Aikichi Kuboyama was among the crew of a Japanese fishing boat accidentally showered with radioactive dust during an American H-bomb test at Bikini Atoll in the Pacific in March 1954. He died of the effects of the radiation.

400 times more powerful than the bombs that had destroyed Japanese cities in 1945. But the US advantage was soon lost again since Soviet nuclear scientists developed their own H-bomb.

NUCLEAR TESTS

Tests of nuclear devices, carried out at remote sites in deserts or on islands, hurled vast quantities of radioactive material into the atmosphere. There was an extraordinary lack of concern over damage to the environment and the effects of radiation. The United States and the Soviet Union agreed to stop aboveground nuclear tests in 1963.

IN THEIR OWN WORDS

US soldier James Yeatts recalled a nuclear test in Nevada:

We had no protective clothing or equipment . . . We turned to see the fireball form. The shockwave hit us and knocked me backward. The dust was so thick we couldn't see anything. After the dust settled we marched toward Ground Zero until the radiation got too hot.

Quoted in Harvey Wasserman and Norman Solomon, *Killing Our Own* by (Delacorte Press, 1982)

THE MISSILE RACE

In addition to racing to create ever bigger nuclear explosions, the United States and the Soviet Union competed to develop ways of launching nuclear strikes against each other's territory. The United States at first concentrated on building long-range bomber aircraft. But it soon became obvious that the best way of deploying nuclear explosives was as warheads on missiles.

ROCKET MEN

During World War II, Nazi Germany developed the world's first ballistic missile, the V-2 rocket. From 1944, V-2s were used to attack London and other targets.

In the final months of the war, as US and Soviet troops overran Germany, there was a race to capture German rocket scientists. The most important scientists, led by Wernher von Braun, surrendered to the United States. Von Braun and his team were taken to the United States to develop missiles for the US Army.

German-born scientist Wernher von Braun (right) shows a model of the missile he designed for the US Army in the 1950s. Von Braun contributed to both US nuclear weapons development and space exploration.

A Soviet postcard celebrates the launch of the world's first artificial satellites, *Sputnik 1* and *2*, in 1957. The rockets used to launch the satellites could also carry nuclear warheads to strike US cities.

STRIKING ACROSS CONTINENTS

Despite this, at first the Soviets did much better than the United States at building missiles. Led by Sergei Korolev, Soviet rocket scientists built the giant R-7, an intercontinental ballistic missile (ICBM) capable of striking US cities with a nuclear warhead.

The world became aware of the R-7's existence in 1957, when it was used to launch *Sputnik 1*, the world's first satellite, into space. The United States, thoroughly alarmed, rushed to catch up. By 1959, both sides had nuclear-armed missiles deployed and ready for use at a moment's notice.

PROLIFERATING MISSILES

A US submarine-launched ballistic missile (SLBM), the Polaris, was first fired in 1960. Cruise missiles—guided flying bombs—with nuclear warheads were deployed on land, on aircraft, and on ships. Scientists also developed multiple warheads so that a single ballistic missile could strike up to 10 different targets. The nuclear powers had 50,000 warheads stockpiled by the 1980s, each one far more powerful than the original atom bomb.

SURVIVAL IN A "MAD" WORLD

The spectacular growth of nuclear arsenals meant the opposing sides in the Cold War had the power to destroy each other's cities and military bases in days, if not hours. This situation was aptly called MAD, standing for Mutually Assured Destruction. Yet by threatening such devastation, nuclear weapons deterred either side from starting a war.

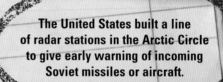

The United States built a line of radar stations in the Arctic Circle to give early warning of incoming Soviet missiles or aircraft.

FIRST STRIKE FEARS

"Nuclear deterrence"—avoiding war by threatening mutual destruction—was a dangerous business. Both sides feared that their enemy would launch a surprise "first strike" to destroy their nuclear weapons before they could respond.

The United States and its allies established an early warning system to keep a 24-hour watch for any sign of an enemy first strike. A far-flung chain of

FALLOUT SHELTERS

Shelters were built for government and military personnel in case of nuclear war. These used concrete and earth to protect against blast and nuclear radiation. Those sheltering would have had to stay inside for at least two weeks to avoid contamination by radioactive dust, or "fallout."

radar stations was linked to an underground command base tunneled deep inside Cheyenne Mountain, Colorado. Spy satellites watched for flashes on Soviet territory that might indicate missiles being launched.

FOUR-MINUTE WARNING

The system would have given time to launch a nuclear missile counterstrike in case of a Soviet attack but left civilians with little hope. In Britain, people would have had four minutes warning of a nuclear attack. There was also a risk of a nuclear war starting by accident. A mistake or malfunction by the radar system, for example, could have triggered the firing of nuclear missiles at any time.

ON THE BRINK

In November 1983, the United States and its allies carried out a military exercise called Able Archer, designed to simulate preparations for a nuclear war. The Soviet Union thought the exercise might be for real and put its nuclear forces on alert. Without the general public knowing anything about it, the world stood on the brink of nuclear war for a week, until the exercise ended.

Thousands of American families bought their own private nuclear fallout shelters in the 1950s and 1960s. Children at school were taught to "duck and cover" in case of nuclear attack—that is, to hide under their desks.

CUBA AND THE MISSILE CRISIS

The nearest that the world has ever come to a nuclear war was in 1962. The flash point was the Caribbean island of Cuba. Fidel Castro, who took power in Cuba in 1959, allied his country with the Soviet Union. Outraged by the presence of a pro-Soviet state only 90 miles (140 kilometers) from their coast, the United States plotted to overthrow Castro. In September 1962, Soviet leader Nikita Khrushchev started secretly installing nuclear missiles on Cuba.

MISSILE SITES

The United States was alerted to the Soviet move by Oleg Penkovsky, a double agent in Soviet military intelligence. The information was confirmed by a U-2 spy plane overflying Cuba, which photographed missile sites under construction. President John F. Kennedy was determined to force the Soviet Union to remove the missiles, which threatened US cities. His military chiefs wanted to launch air strikes to destroy the missile sites, but Kennedy

Photographs taken by U-2 spy planes revealed launch sites for Soviet missiles being built on Cuba. It required expert analysis to work out what the aerial photos actually showed.

SOVIET DOUBLE AGENT

Soviet intelligence officer Oleg Penkovsky became a double agent in 1961, passing secrets to the CIA and SIS. In September 1962, he revealed to them that the Soviet Union was stationing nuclear missiles in Cuba. The following month, Penkovsky was arrested by the KGB. He was executed as a traitor, killed by a single bullet in the back of the neck.

Former Soviet intelligence officer Oleg Penkovsky hears his death sentence, convicted of betraying the Soviet Union by telling the Americans about the stationing of missiles in Cuba.

feared this would lead to a nuclear war. Instead, he put Cuba under naval blockade and called on Khrushchev to withdraw the missiles.

STANDOFF

While the two sides secretly negotiated in search of a solution to the crisis, tension neared breaking point. A U-2 spy plane was shot down over Cuba, and there were close encounters between US and Soviet ships and submarines. After a standoff lasting 13 days, Khrushchev announced that the missiles were being withdrawn. Kennedy responded by promising that the United States would never invade Cuba.

IN THEIR OWN WORDS

At the height of the Cuban missile crisis, philosopher and anti-nuclear campaigner Bertrand Russell wrote:

I urge every human being who loves life to come out in the streets of our country and demonstrate our demand to live and let live. There must not be war.

Quoted in Ray Monk, *Bertrand Russell: The Ghost of Madness* (Vintage, 2001)

PREPARING FOR THE THIRD WORLD WAR

For 40 years, both sides in the Cold War made plans to fight a third world war. They constantly updated their technology and their tactics, looking for secret and stealthy ways to get the edge over their opponents if a global war was ever fought. This led to the development of some truly terrifying weapons.

The Neutron Bomb One Step Closer to DOOMSDAY!

Anti-nuclear protesters simulate the deadly effect of a neutron bomb.

CHEMICAL AND BIOLOGICAL WEAPONS

Armies on both sides had stocks of deadly chemicals, including nerve agents such as sarin. Contact with a tiny droplet of sarin can kill a person in less than a minute. There were also plans to use biological weapons—for example, to

SECRET ARMIES

NATO war preparations included preparing "stay-behind" networks to continue fighting in countries that had been conquered by the Soviet army. These secret armies would have carried out sabotage attacks against Soviet occupation forces, getting weapons from hidden arms dumps.

COLD WAR DOLPHINS

Both the United States and the Soviet Union trained dolphins to serve as Cold War warriors. Dolphins were able to search for enemy mines in the ocean using their natural sonar echolocation faculty. Dolphins were also trained to attach explosive charges to the hulls of enemy ships.

A dolphin trained by the US Navy locates a hostile torpedo on the seabed.

infect the enemy with spores of the killer disease anthrax. The United States destroyed its biological weapons in 1972, but the Soviet Union continued to store and develop them secretly.

BATTLEFIELD NUKES

Both sides had tactical nuclear weapons—small nuclear devices designed for use against enemy armed forces on the battlefield. These could be fired as artillery shells, dropped as bombs, or deployed as missile warheads.

The creepiest of tactical nuclear devices was the neutron bomb, which would kill people without damaging buildings or hardware. The radiation would pass straight through the armor of a tank or a concrete wall, leaving them intact, but kill the people inside.

WONDER WEAPONS

The development of military technology was astounding. For example, by the 1980s some military jets could fly as fast as a rifle bullet—about three times the speed of sound. Machines such as nuclear-powered submarines and Stealth aircraft—designed to be undetectable by radar—were wonders of the world.

AGENTS AND SPY CATCHERS

Throughout the Cold War, secret services fought a shadowy conflict, the workings of which were only occasionally revealed to the general public. Intelligence officers ran networks of secret agents in hostile countries and organized armed subversion or even assassinations. Their efforts were opposed by counterespionage and surveillance experts dedicated to rooting out spies and alleged subversives.

SECRET SERVICES

When the Cold War started, the Soviet Union definitely had the largest, most powerful secret service. Then called the NKVD, and later renamed the KGB, it combined an all-powerful secret police at home with a far-flung spying network abroad.

The United States had the long-established Federal Bureau of Investigation (FBI) to counter espionage and subversion. In 1947, the United States set up the Central Intelligence Agency (CIA) to carry out intelligence gathering, espionage, and other "covert operations"

THE PROFUMO AFFAIR

In 1963, the British public learned that their Secretary of State for War, John Profumo, had been having an affair with a young woman, Christine Keeler. She was also sleeping with a Russian from the Soviet embassy in London, Captain Yevgeny Ivanov. Like most Soviet embassy personnel, Ivanov was a spy. Many feared that British defense secrets had been leaked to the Soviets. There was a huge scandal, and Profumo had to resign.

JAMES ANGLETON

The CIA's chief spy catcher from the 1950s to the 1970s was James Angleton. He became obsessed with the idea that the CIA had been penetrated by Soviet double agents. He even believed British prime minister Harold Wilson was a Soviet agent. Angleton described the spy world as a "wilderness of mirrors," where it was impossible to tell truth from lies.

Truckloads of shredded CIA documents are dumped every day, a product of the organization's obsession with secrecy.

abroad. These might range from training anti-communist guerrillas to arranging the overthrow of foreign heads of state.

SUSPICION AND DISTRUST

These secret organizations grew to an astonishing size in the Cold War—by the 1980s, the CIA employed over 16,000 people and spent $1.5 billion a year. Its tentacles spread everywhere. It recruited agents in foreign governments, including double agents in its enemies' secret services. Embassies became centers of espionage, the "diplomats" in fact engaged in secret intelligence gathering. The result was a general atmosphere of suspicion and distrust.

Christine Keeler, an attractive young woman out for a good time, accidentally became caught up in Cold War espionage and political scandal.

THE ATOM SPIES

When the Soviet Union exploded its first atom bomb in 1949, shocked and fearful Americans looked for someone to blame. Although Soviet scientists had in fact mostly worked out how to build the bomb for themselves, the Soviet Union did have spies gathering information on the US atomic weapons program. These "atom spies" became the United States' most notorious public enemies.

PASSING ON SECRETS

Some of the scientists recruited by the United States for the atom bomb project in World War II were sympathetic to the Soviet Union. These scientists, including physicists Klaus Fuchs and Allan Nunn May, were easily persuaded to pass on atomic secrets to Soviet spies.

Western intelligence agencies made their first breakthrough in 1946. Using information provided by Igor Gouzenko, a clerk at the Soviet embassy in Canada, they identified Nunn May as a spy. Fuchs was not picked up until four years later. He was identified when US and British

German physicist Klaus Fuchs fled from Germany to Britain in 1933 to escape the Nazis. A committed communist, he passed details of British and US nuclear weapons development to the Soviet Union for a decade before his arrest in 1950.

IN THEIR OWN WORDS

President Dwight D. Eisenhower explained why he refused to grant the Rosenbergs a reprieve from execution:

By immeasurably increasing the chances of atomic war, the Rosenbergs may have condemned to death tens of millions of innocent people all over the world. The execution of two human beings is a grave matter. But even graver is the thought of millions of dead, whose death may be directly attributable to what these spies have done.

Guardian, June 20, 1953

Ethel and Julius Rosenberg, on trial as Soviet spies, embrace while handcuffed together in a prison van. They had passed on secrets from Ethel's brother David Greenglass, who worked for the Manhattan Project.

code breakers succeeded in cracking some Soviet intelligence messages they had intercepted.

SPY RING EXPOSED

The interrogation of Fuchs led to Harry Gold, the Soviet agent he had passed information to in the United States. Gold's testimony identified Julius Rosenberg and his brother-in-law David Greenglass as other members of the spy ring.

Catching the atom spies was undoubtedly a success for the US and British counterespionage services, but the revelation of their activities generally made people feel more insecure, fearing hidden enemies in their midst.

ATOM SPIES EXECUTED

Julius Rosenberg and his wife, Ethel, were Jewish Americans. Although small fry in the spying business, a US court condemned them to death in the electric chair. Other atom spies were only given long prison terms. There were worldwide protests against the executions, which were carried out on June 19, 1953.

21

THE BRITISH MOLES

A "mole" is an agent buried inside the enemy's secret services, working on behalf of a foreign power. Soviet moles were especially successful in Britain during the Cold War, occupying important positions with access to top-secret information. The unmasking of these long-term double agents caused shock and scandal.

THE CAMBRIDGE SPIES

The British moles were men from privileged backgrounds. They were recruited by the Soviet secret service while at Cambridge University in the 1930s, at a time when belief in communism was fashionable. Because they were members of the ruling class, they later had no difficulty getting jobs in British secret agencies or the foreign office. One of them, Kim Philby, became a leading officer in the SIS. Another, Donald Maclean, became a senior diplomat.

Guy Burgess—heavy drinking made him an unreliable spy.

Donald Maclean, British diplomat who gave Moscow high-level secrets.

ESCAPE TO THE SOVIET UNION

US counterintelligence eventually became suspicious of Maclean. In 1951, tipped off by Philby, Maclean disappeared from Britain just in time to avoid arrest, accompanied by fellow spy Guy Burgess. The pair resurfaced in the Soviet Union. Philby came under suspicion as a result of their disappearance and was dismissed from his job. Left at liberty, he later also escaped to Moscow.

The British moles revealed important secrets to the Soviet Union. Philby in particular betrayed many agents working for the West in communist countries. There were repeated rumors that other moles remained undiscovered. In fact, two more "Cambridge spies" were identified: Anthony Blunt (see panel) and John Cairncross.

THE QUEEN'S SPY

In 1979, it was revealed that Sir Anthony Blunt, an art historian, had been a Soviet agent while working for the British intelligence services in the 1940s. Blunt was at one time the Keeper of the Queen's Pictures—the man responsible for the royal art collection. The queen stripped him of his knighthood after he was revealed as a spy.

Anthony Blunt, the queen's art expert and a spy.

Kim Philby, Soviet spy in the SIS.

IN THEIR OWN WORDS

Soviet agent Kim Philby wrote about how easy it was for him to get a job in the British secret service:

The only enquiry made into my past was the routine reference to MI5, who passed my name through their records and came back with the statement: "Nothing recorded against."

From Kim Philby, *My Silent War* (MacGibbon & Kee, 1968)

BERLIN: DIVIDED CITY

The German city of Berlin was sometimes called "the capital of the Cold War." For many years, it was the only "hole" in the Iron Curtain—the only place in Europe where people could move freely between East and West.

In October 1961, US tanks faced Soviet tanks on opposite sides of Checkpoint Charlie, a crossing point in the Berlin Wall.

FOUR SECTORS

Berlin was inside communist East Germany, but the city was divided into four sectors occupied by Soviet, US, British, and French troops. This odd arrangement, made at the end of World War II, lasted for over 40 years. The US, British, and French sectors were known as West Berlin and the Soviet sector as East Berlin.

CITY OF SPIES

In 1948–1949, the Soviet Union tried to force the Western allies out of the city by blocking the land routes to West Berlin.

BUILDING THE WALL

The building of the Berlin Wall began without warning on the night of August 12–13, 1961. Panicking East Germans made desperate attempts to escape, some jumping from upstairs windows in buildings in the East to land in the West. US and Soviet tanks faced up to one another on opposite sides of the wall, but no shots were fired.

The US and British air forces kept Berlin supplied by an airlift and the Soviet blockade failed.

In the 1950s, it was easy to cross between East and West Berlin—people even lived on one side and worked on the other. Spying flourished, with agents and informers congregating in cafés to buy and sell information.

THE WALL

In 1961, the Soviets decided free movement had to stop. They built a wall between East and West Berlin, patrolled by soldiers and police with guns and dogs. The wall cut across streets, dividing families and neighborhoods.

Thousands of people in the East sought to escape. They dug tunnels, crawled through sewers, or simply tried to climb over the wall at night. More than a hundred were killed making the attempt.

GREAT ESCAPE

In 1964, a group of students dug a tunnel from an outside toilet in a courtyard in East Berlin under the wall to a bakery in West Berlin. The tunnel was 476 feet (145 meters) long and took six months to dig. In the end, 57 people crawled through the tunnel to the West, the largest mass escape in the wall's history.

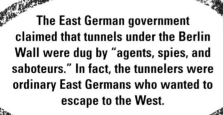

The East German government claimed that tunnels under the Berlin Wall were dug by "agents, spies, and saboteurs." In fact, the tunnelers were ordinary East Germans who wanted to escape to the West.

TOOLS OF THE TRADE

The Cold War rivals developed an ingenious array of gadgets and gizmos for the business of espionage. At first, most of these were for the use of secret agents. Over time, though, surveillance satellites and communication intercepts became more vital to intelligence work than agents on the ground.

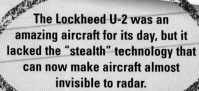

The Lockheed U-2 was an amazing aircraft for its day, but it lacked the "stealth" technology that can now make aircraft almost invisible to radar.

SECRET DOCUMENTS

A Cold War–era secret agent would typically carry a camera that fit into a matchbox. He used this to photograph secret documents onto microfilm. The photographs were so small that hundreds of them could be hidden in a container such as a toothpaste tube or a hollowed-out electric battery.

LOCKHEED U-2 SPY PLANE

The CIA began secret flights over the Soviet Union with a high-altitude spy plane, the U-2, in 1956. The aircraft's cameras could photograph the ground in detail from a height of 68,900 feet (21,000 meters). Two U-2s were shot down by surface-to-air missiles, however, and from the 1960s, their job was mostly taken over by satellites.

The secret agent would have a one-time code pad for encoding messages that could only be read by another person with the same pad—a sheet was torn off each time the pad was used. The message might be hidden in an apparently ordinary letter by the microdot technique, the whole message shrunk to the size of a period.

LISTENING TO THE ENEMY

Bugging played a large part in espionage. At foreign embassies, listening devices (or bugs) were hidden in walls, window frames, telephone receivers, and ornaments. Counterespionage personnel

BERLIN TUNNEL

The largest bugging exercise ever undertaken was a US-British project to tap the telephone line between the Soviet military headquarters in Berlin and Moscow. In 1955, the CIA and SIS dug a tunnel under the Soviet sector of Berlin to reach the phone line. But the tunnel project ended in failure because as it was betrayed to the KGB by a double agent inside the SIS, George Blake.

regularly "swept" embassy buildings to identify bugs. Diplomats held their most secret conversations in bug-proof boxes inside rooms.

Both sides listened in to enemy radio messages, but all secret messages were encoded, and these codes could rarely be cracked—even using powerful computers. At best, cryptographers were able to decipher only one in a hundred top-secret messages.

Miniaturized listening devices could be hidden anywhere in a room, such as behind a picture frame.

SECRET MISSIONS

The Cold War secret services organized undercover operations ranging from intelligence gathering to assassination. The principle of "deniability" was the key—if things did not work out, the secret services needed to be able to deny that they had anything to do with it. The public mostly only heard about these secret missions when something went wrong.

British diver Buster Crabb (left) prepares for a mission. Crabb disappeared while carrying out an operation for the British secret service in 1956.

BUSTER CRABB

One embarrassing failed mission occurred in 1956, during an official visit to Britain by Soviet leaders. A diver, Lionel "Buster" Crabb, was sent by the SIS to examine the hull of the cruiser the visitors had traveled in. He dived into Portsmouth harbor, where the cruiser was moored, and vanished. Fourteen months later, a headless corpse, which may have been Crabb, washed up on a nearby shore. Whether or not the Soviets killed him is still unknown.

GARY POWERS

In May 1960, US pilot Gary Powers was employed by the CIA to fly a U-2 spy

SPY SWAP

The Soviet authorities sentenced captured US pilot Gary Powers to 10 years in prison. But he was released in 1962 when the United States agreed to a "spy swap." They were holding a KGB officer, Rudolf Abel, who had been caught spying in the United States. Abel was exchanged for Powers at the Glienicke Bridge in Berlin.

After his release from a Soviet prison, U-2 pilot Gary Powers had to testify in front of a US Senate committee about his failed mission.

plane over the Soviet Union. His plane was shot down, and Powers was captured by the Soviets. They waited until the US government had publicly denied carrying out spy flights, then revealed Powers to the world, proving the US government was lying.

ASSASSINS

The greatest secrecy surrounds the work of assassins. We know, for example, that the CIA plotted to assassinate Cuban leader Fidel Castro, but the plots came to nothing. Some believe that agents from communist Bulgaria, working on behalf of the Soviet Union, arranged the attempted assassination of Pope John Paul II in 1981, but evidence is scarce.

THE UMBRELLA ASSASSIN

Georgi Markov was a well-known Bulgarian dissident living in London. In 1978, while standing at a bus stop, he felt a sharp pain in his leg. He had been stabbed with the point of an umbrella. The umbrella was used by a Bulgarian secret agent to inject a poison capsule into his body. Markov died in agony four days later.

ENEMIES WITHIN

When the Cold War started, the Soviet Union, ruled by dictator Joseph Stalin, was a ruthless police state that held millions of its people in prison camps for allegedly opposing the government. The United States and its allies allowed their citizens far greater freedom, but even they clamped down on internal opposition during the Cold War.

BLACKLIST

In the United States, a crackdown on alleged communist sympathizers began in 1947 with a focus on the movie industry. Hundreds of actors and screenwriters were put on a "blacklist," in effect banning them from working in Hollywood.

McCARTHYISM

In 1950, Senator Joseph McCarthy declared that many government employees were in fact communists. He gave his name to "McCarthyism," under which thousands of US citizens were fired from their jobs or arrested on the flimsiest evidence. People were put under intense pressure to betray their friends and colleagues. McCarthyism fizzled out from the mid-1950s, but the FBI continued to target supposed subversives until the 1970s.

Joe McCarthy, senator for Wisconsin, made himself the spokesman for extreme anti-communism at the height of the Cold War. He claimed the United States was threatened by communist traitors in government.

IN THEIR OWN WORDS

Edward Murrow, a famous US journalist, called for an end to McCarthyism in a TV broadcast in 1954. He stated:

We must not confuse dissent with disloyalty. We must remember that accusation is not proof . . . We will not walk in fear, one of another.

Edward R. Murrow: A Report on Senator Joseph R. McCarthy. *See It Now* (CBS-TV, March 9, 1954)

Soviet dissidents, including Vladimir Bukovsky (second from right), who survived 12 years in Soviet labor camps and mental hospitals, and Edward Kuznetsov (second from left), who tried to hijack an aircraft to escape to the West in 1970.

POLITICAL PRISONERS

In the Soviet Union, Stalin's death in 1953 was followed by the release of most prison camp inmates. But the Soviet state continued to persecute dissidents—anyone who called for freedom, democracy, and human rights. Instead of sending them to prison, the Soviet authorities took to committing their opponents to mental hospitals, claiming they were insane.

Dissidents could not publish their views in books or newspapers because of state censorship, but they circulated information secretly from hand to hand. Anyone caught with such "samizdat" documents faced harsh punishment. The persecution of dissidents only ended after liberal Soviet leader Mikhail Gorbachev took over in 1985.

ANDREI SAKHAROV

Scientist Andrei Sakharov helped create the Soviet hydrogen bomb in the 1950s. Later, Sakharov became a dissident. He spoke out in favor of human rights and against aggressive Soviet policies such as the invasion of Afghanistan in 1979. For this, he was punished by being sent to the remote city of Gorky, where he lived for six years under close police surveillance.

BACKYARD PROBLEMS

During the Cold War, both the United States and the Soviet Union had problems in areas close to home—in their own backyards. The peoples of Eastern Europe were often resentful of the communist governments imposed on them by Soviet power. In the Caribbean and in Central and South America, popular movements opposed US-backed regimes.

EASTERN EUROPE

In 1956, Hungarians revolted against the Soviet-backed government. They armed themselves, fought the secret police, and demanded political change. A new government promised to hold democratic elections and end Hungary's alliance with the Soviet Union. But in October, the Soviet army invaded Hungary and crushed the revolt. More than 3,000 people died in the fighting.

In 1968, the Czechoslovak government, led by Alexander Dubcek, announced liberal reforms. There was a peaceful

THE INVASION OF CZECHOSLOVAKIA

On the night of August 20, 1968, a flight from Moscow landed at an airport in the Czech capital, Prague. A hundred armed Soviet agents in plainclothes left the aircraft and seized the airport. Thousands of Soviet troops were then flown in, while tanks drove across the country's borders. The Czechs mostly protested peacefully against the invasion, knowing resistance would be futile.

celebration of the new freedoms in the "Prague Spring." But in autumn, the Soviets once again sent in the tanks and reimposed hard-line communism.

CENTRAL AND SOUTH AMERICA

The United States repeatedly intervened to support anti-communist governments or undermine communist governments in its backyard. The CIA played a murky role in the overthrow of the democratically elected government of Guatemala in 1953 and of Chile in 1973. US troops were sent into the Dominican Republic in 1964 and Grenada in 1983. Determined to prevent the spread of communism, the United States supported dictatorships that used torture and murder to stay in power.

In 1983, US troops invaded the Caribbean island of Grenada, an independent country in the British Commonwealth. US military intervention ended Grenada's close relations with Cuba and installed a pro-American government in power.

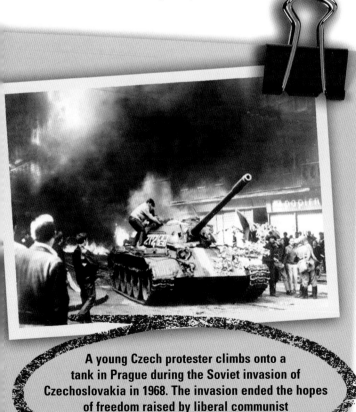

A young Czech protester climbs onto a tank in Prague during the Soviet invasion of Czechoslovakia in 1968. The invasion ended the hopes of freedom raised by liberal communist Alexander Dubcek.

IN THEIR OWN WORDS

The United States never accepted that people in South America had a right to elect an anti-American government. In 1970, when the people of Chile seemed likely to vote in large numbers for the communist party, Secretary of State Henry Kissinger said:

I don't see why we need to stand by and watch a country go communist because of the irresponsibility of its own people.

Henry Kissinger at a meeting of the US National Security Council's 40 Committee, June 27, 1970

GUERRILLAS AND REVOLUTIONARIES

The Cold War confrontation between the United States and the Soviet Union became mixed up with many local struggles across the world. The Soviets supported movements fighting for national liberation from the rule of European colonial powers or against oppressive and corrupt governments backed by the United States.

IN MAO'S FOOTSTEPS

The example for revolutionary guerrilla war was set by Mao Ze Dong in China. Starting as the leader of an armed band of communists in the Chinese countryside, Mao built up his movement until he defeated the US-backed Chinese Nationalist government in 1949, making China a communist state. Mao's success was an inspiration to other movements resisting unpopular dictators or rule by foreign colonial powers.

Fidel Castro (left) and "Che" Guevara saw their guerrilla war in Cuba as part of a worldwide struggle against US imperialism.

FIDEL AND CHE

Bearded rebel Fidel Castro launched a guerrilla campaign in a remote part of rural Cuba with just 81 armed followers. After three years' fighting, he

Vietnamese peasant children prepare a booby trap of sharp bamboo spikes, designed to injure US soldiers on patrol during the Vietnam War.

overthrew Cuban dictator Fulgencio Batista in 1959. Castro declared himself a communist and allied Cuba with the Soviet Union. Castro's Argentinian colleague Ernesto "Che" Guevara hoped to ignite additional guerrilla wars around the world, but in 1967, he and his small band of fighters were defeated in Bolivia. Guevara was shot dead.

SOUTHEAST ASIA

In Southeast Asia, Vietnamese communists fought successful guerrilla wars first against the French and then against the United States and pro-US Vietnamese. By 1975, all of Vietnam and neighboring Cambodia and Laos had communist governments. These communist victories were severe setbacks for the United States in the Cold War, extending the area of influence of the Soviet Union and China.

THE AK-47 RIFLE

The most famous weapon used by guerrillas was the Soviet-manufactured AK-47 assault rifle. Designed by Russian Mikhail Kalashnikov in the 1940s, the AK-47 was tough, easy to use, cheap to produce, and deadly. Millions of the rifles were manufactured by the Soviet Union and other communist countries and distributed to liberation movements they supported.

35

HIDDEN WAR IN VIETNAM

In the 1960s, the United States became involved in a major conflict in Southeast Asia. US aircraft bombed communist-ruled North Vietnam, and hundreds of thousands of US soldiers were deployed against communist-led guerrillas in South Vietnam. In parallel with these large-scale military operations, a ruthless secret war was fought by the CIA and US Army Special Forces.

A US Special Forces officer leads Montagnard fighters on a jungle patrol in the Vietnam War.

A-TEAMS

The US Army Special Forces, or "Green Berets," were elite soldiers trained to operate in small groups behind enemy lines. In 1962, Green Beret "A-Teams" were sent into villages deep inside enemy lines. They trained and armed the mountain people—the "Montagnards"—

PEOPLE SPOTTING

US scientists invented ingenious gadgets to spot guerrillas moving through the Vietnamese jungle. Listening devices were dropped by parachute to hang in the jungle canopy. Other sensors, disguised as tiny plants on the forest floor, registered the shaking of the earth when men walked past. US helicopters carried "people sniffers," devices that detected the body odor of a person on the ground below.

as jungle fighters and led them in a campaign of ambushes and surprise attacks against communist bases, taking on the guerrillas at their own game.

OPERATIONS IN LAOS

The CIA ran its own secret war in Laos, a country bordering Vietnam and used by the North Vietnamese as a route for sending men and weapons to the guerrillas in the south. The CIA organized and supplied anti-communist forces in Laos. To cover up the operation, it flew in men and supplies using a civilian airline, Air America, which it secretly owned.

PHOENIX PROGRAM

The CIA also played a large part in the Phoenix Program. This was an attempt to eradicate communist influence in South Vietnamese villages by identifying and targeting communist villagers. Often alleged communists were simply killed. At the same time, communist agents murdered thousands of villagers they considered pro-American.

FLIGHT FROM SAIGON

US troops withdrew from Vietnam by 1973, but the CIA remained in South Vietnam. In 1975, North Vietnamese tanks overran the south. As the tanks entered the South Vietnamese capital, Saigon, CIA and other US personnel, along with thousands of Vietnamese who had worked for the United States, were lifted out by helicopter to ships offshore.

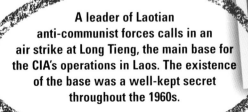

A leader of Laotian anti-communist forces calls in an air strike at Long Tieng, the main base for the CIA's operations in Laos. The existence of the base was a well-kept secret throughout the 1960s.

US-BACKED REBELS

During the Cold War, the CIA armed and trained rebel groups to fight against communist or anti-American governments. US-backed rebel movements fought guerrilla wars in many places, including Nicaragua, Angola, and Afghanistan. These operations led the CIA into many murky dealings.

American-backed Contra guerrillas in Nicaragua.

NICARAGUA

In Nicaragua, the Sandinista movement took power after a successful guerrilla war in 1979. The United States regarded the Sandinistas as pro-communist. The CIA organized and armed a group of anti-Sandinista Nicaraguans known as the "Contras," who waged a brutal war against the Sandinista government and its supporters. The Sandinistas lost power in Nicaragua in 1990.

BAY OF PIGS

In April 1961, Cuban exiles—people who had fled Cuba after Fidel Castro installed a communist government—attempted to invade Cuba and overthrow Castro. They had been recruited and trained by the CIA. The United States also supplied them with bomber aircraft and ships. The invaders landed at the Bay of Pigs in southern Cuba but were swiftly overwhelmed by Castro's forces. All were killed or captured.

ANGOLA

Angola was another focus for Cold War conflict. From 1975, Angola's government was supported by the Soviet Union and Cuba, while rebel UNITA guerrillas were backed by the United States and South Africa (then under an all-white government). The Angolan civil war, which devastated the country, continued long after the Cold War, ending in 2002.

AFGHANISTAN

In Afghanistan, the CIA encouraged Muslim mujahideen tribal fighters to rebel against the pro-Soviet Afghan government. In December 1979, Soviet troops invaded Afghanistan to resist the tribal rebellion. The United States supplied the mujahideen and Islamic extremists from outside Afghanistan with weapons and money to fight the Soviets. The Soviet Union was eventually forced to admit defeat and withdraw from Afghanistan after a decade of very costly warfare.

IN THEIR OWN WORDS

Zbigniew Brzezinski, National Security Adviser to President Jimmy Carter in 1979, later defended the decision to give US support to Islamic extremists fighting Soviet troops in Afghanistan. He said:

What is more important to the history of the world? Some stirred-up Muslims or the liberation of Central Europe and the end of the Cold War?

Brzezinski in interview with *Nouvel Observateur* magazine, 1998

A mujahideen fighter in Afghanistan uses a rocket-propelled grenade launcher during the war against the Soviet invaders in the 1980s.

PROPAGANDA AND PRESTIGE

Instead of fighting with guns and bombs, the two sides in the Cold War spent a lot of time fighting with words and images. In this propaganda conflict, each side set out to show that its system worked best. They competed in every area of life, from sports to space exploration.

SPORTS

Every Olympic Games in the Cold War era became a trial of strength between East and West. The temptation to cheat was strong. Communist East Germany regularly doped its athletes with steroids to achieve medal-winning performances.

CHESS BATTLES

The Cold War was even fought on chessboards. In 1972, the defeat of Soviet champion Boris Spassky by American Bobby Fischer was hailed as a triumph for the West.

When US chess player Bobby Fischer (right) beat Soviet grand master Boris Spassky in 1972, he became the first American to hold the title of World Chess Champion in the 20th century.

SPACE

The space race was the most extreme example of Cold War competition. The Soviet Union won immense prestige for putting the first satellite in space in 1957 and, above all, for the first manned space flight in 1961. The United States responded by putting enormous resources behind the Apollo project, which aimed to land a man on the moon. The successful moon landing in 1969 made the United States victors in space, although at a high price—about $25 billion (equivalent to $140 billion today).

The annual May Day parade in Moscow was always an occasion to show off Soviet military might and engage in anti-American propaganda. These floats in 1970 celebrate Vietnamese communist resistance to US bombs.

CULTURE WARS

Soviet propagandists accurately highlighted the existence of poverty, crime, and racism in Western societies. In much of the world, their accusation that the United States was "imperialist" pressed the right buttons. But the United States had the advantage of a higher standard of living and vibrant popular culture. Hollywood movies and pop records, jeans and cans of Coke were, in the end, the best propaganda for the American way of life.

IN THEIR OWN WORDS

Speaking in September 1962, President John F. Kennedy specifically linked the US space program to the United States' desire for world leadership:

The exploration of space . . . is one of the great adventures of all time, and no nation that expects to be the leader of other nations can expect to stay behind in the race for space.

Kennedy address at Rice University, September 12, 1962

THE END OF THE COLD WAR

In 1983, the United States was controversially stationing Pershing Cruise missiles in Europe and the Soviets were fighting a war in Afghanistan. The Cold War looked set to last forever. The astonishing turnaround that brought the Cold War to an end was triggered by a new Soviet leader, Mikhail Gorbachev.

FALL OF THE BERLIN WALL

The wall between East and West Berlin was a key symbol of the Cold War and the Iron Curtain division of Europe. In November 1989, the communist East German government, faced with mass protests against its rule, was forced to let people cross the wall. There were wild celebrations as East Berliners met West Berliners. The demolition of the wall began the following year.

East Germans help one another to climb onto the Berlin Wall in November 1989 after the border between the two halves of the city was opened. East and West Germany were reunited in October 1990.

AN END TO CONFRONTATION

After coming to power in 1985, Gorbachev set out to reform the Soviet system and improve relations with the West. At a series of summit meetings with President Ronald Reagan, Gorbachev pushed for radical cuts in nuclear weapons.

Reagan had called the Soviet Union an "evil empire" and was planning a "Star Wars" defense system to protect the United States against nuclear attack using space-based anti-missile missiles. Despite his anti-communism, however, Reagan came to accept that Gorbachev's desire for an end to Cold War hostility was genuine. In 1987, a treaty reducing nuclear arsenals was signed. The following year, Soviet troops were withdrawn from Afghanistan.

THE COLLAPSE OF COMMUNISM

Gorbachev hoped to strengthen communism by reforming it, but once people were given more freedom, the communist system began to collapse. Gorbachev announced that Soviet tanks would no longer be sent to support communist governments in Eastern Europe. In 1989, people in Poland, East Germany, Romania, Hungary, and Czechoslovakia overthrew communist regimes, opting for Western-style democracy.

The Iron Curtain disappeared, and the Cold War came to an end. Within two years, communism also collapsed in the Soviet Union, which ceased to exist.

President Ronald Reagan (left) and Soviet leader Mikhail Gorbachev developed a positive relationship that let them negotiate an end to the Cold War.

IN THEIR OWN WORDS

Mikhail Gorbachev, the last leader of the Soviet Union, later talked of the cost of the Cold War to both the United States and the Soviet Union:

I think we all lost the Cold War, particularly the Soviet Union. We each lost $10 trillion . . . We only won when the Cold War ended.

Interview with Robert G. Kaiser, *Washington Post,* June 11, 2004

TIMELINE

March 12, 1947 President Harry S. Truman promises to resist communism worldwide.

June 25, 1950 Communist North Korean troops invade South Korea, starting the Korean War.

August 29, 1949 The Soviet Union carries out its first atom bomb test.

May 25, 1951 Soviet spies Guy Burgess and Donald Maclean flee Britain for Moscow.

November 1, 1952 The United States explodes the first hydrogen bomb.

June 19, 1953 The Rosenbergs are executed as Soviet spies.

November 4, 1956 Soviet troops invade Hungary to suppress an anti-communist uprising.

May 1, 1960 A US spy plane piloted by Gary Powers is shot down over the Soviet Union.

August 12–13, 1961 Construction of the Berlin Wall begins, dividing the city in two.

October 1962 The Cuban Missile Crisis brings the world to the brink of nuclear war.

March 8, 1965 The United States sends marines to fight communist-led guerrillas in Vietnam.

August 20, 1968 The Soviet Union and its allies invade Czechoslovakia to halt liberal reforms.

December 24, 1979 Soviet troops invade Afghanistan.

December 8, 1987 The signing of a nuclear arms treaty signals the end of hostile relations between the United States and the Soviet Union.

November 9, 1989 Gates in the Berlin Wall are opened as communism collapses in Eastern Europe.

December 25, 1991 The Soviet Union ceases to exist.

GLOSSARY

atom bomb A bomb in which the explosion is made by splitting the atom, a process known as nuclear fission.

ballistic missile A missile that is propelled into a high trajectory by a rocket and then returns to earth in free fall.

CIA Central Intelligence Agency: a US organization committed to espionage and other secret operations abroad.

communism A political system involving rule by a single political party and the control of economic life by the state.

Contras US-backed groups opposed to the Sandinista government in Nicaragua.

cruise missile A low-flying, relatively slow, jet-propelled missile with an explosive warhead.

cryptographer An expert in creating or unscrambling secret codes.

Czechoslovakia A country made up of what are now the Czech Republic and Slovakia.

democracy A political system in which the government is elected by the people.

dissident Somebody who publicly disagrees with an established political system or regime.

double agent A spy who appears to work for one side while actually working for the other.

fallout Harmful radioactive dust that falls to the ground after a nuclear explosion.

FBI Federal Bureau of Investigation: the US government agency responsible for internal security and counterintelligence.

guerrilla A soldier who is not part of a regular army and uses ambush and hit-and-run tactics.

hydrogen bomb A bomb in which the explosion is made by crushing atoms together, a process known as nuclear fusion.

intelligence Information, often secret, about an enemy's forces and plans.

Iron Curtain A term for the fortified border dividing communist Eastern Europe from Western Europe during the Cold War.

KGB The Soviet Union's Committee for State Security, responsible for spying abroad and the secret police at home.

McCarthyism Named after Senator Joe McCarthy, a ruthless witch hunt for alleged communists in the United States in the 1950s.

MI5 Military Intelligence Section 5: the British government agency responsible for internal security and counterintelligence.

mole A spy buried inside (working within) the enemy's secret service.

mujahideen A Muslim guerrilla fighter, especially in Afghanistan.

nerve agent A gas or liquid that kills by attacking the human nervous system.

nuclear radiation Harmful particles and rays released in a nuclear explosion.

nuclear weapons Bombs or missiles that release nuclear energy to create a massive explosion—for example, an atom bomb or hydrogen bomb.

samizdat The term for a book or pamphlet secretly circulated among dissidents in the Soviet Union.

SIS Secret Intelligence Service: the British organization for espionage and other covert operations abroad.

Soviet Union Officially known as the Union of Soviet Socialist Republics (USSR), a communist-ruled federation of 15 republics, dominated by Russia.

special forces Elite military personnel skilled in operating behind enemy lines and using guerrilla tactics.

warhead An explosive device fitted to the nose of a missile.

FURTHER INFORMATION

BOOKS
Denega, Danielle M. *24/7: Science Behind the Scenes: Spy Files: The Cold War Pigeon Patrols And Other Animal Spies*. Children's Press, 2007.

Grant, Reg. *Timelines: The Cold War*. Franklin Watts, 2007.

Harrison, Paul. *How Did it Happen? The Cold War*. Franklin Watts, 2005.

Keeley, Jennifer. *American War Library: The Cold War: Espionage*. Lucent Books, 2003.

Price, Sean. *American History Through Primary Sources: Top Secret: Spy Equipment and the Cold War*. Heinemann Library, 2006.

Sheehan, Sean. *Questioning History: The Cold War*. Wayland, 2003.

Walker, Lesley. *On the Front Line: Spying in the Cold War*. Raintree Publishers, 2005.

WEBSITES
www.historylearningsite.co.uk/spies_cold_war.htm

www.bbc.co.uk/history/worldwars/coldwar/

www.nasm.si.edu/exhibitions/gal114/index.htm

news.bbc.co.uk/onthisday/hi/themes/world_politics/cold_war/default.stm

INDEX

Page numbers in **bold** refer to illustrations.